T.H. MEYER wa
He is the founc
Verlag, Basel, a...
journals *Der Europäer* and *The Present Age*. He is the author of several books including *Milestones*; *In the Sign of Five*; *Ludwig Polzer-Hoditz, A Biography*; *D.N. Dunlop, A Biography*; *Rudolf Steiner's Core Mission*; *The Bodhisattva Question*; *Clairvoyance and Consciousness* and *Reality, Truth and Evil*. He is also the editor of *Light for the New Millennium*. Meyer has written numerous articles and gives seminars and lectures around the world.

BAREFOOT THROUGH BURNING LAVA

*On Sicily, the Island of Cain
An Esoteric Travelogue*

T. H. Meyer

TEMPLE LODGE

For Carmelo Samonà

Temple Lodge Publishing Ltd.
Hillside House, The Square
Forest Row, RH18 5ES

www.templelodge.com

First published in English by Temple Lodge Publishing, 2016

Originally published in German under the title *Barfuß durch glühende Lava* by Perseus Verlag, Basel, 2015

Translated by Matthew Barton

© Perseus Verlag 2015
This translation © Temple Lodge Publishing 2016

The Publishers are grateful to the Perseus Förderverein for their generous sponsorship of the translation

This book is copyright under the Berne Convention. All rights reserved. Apart from any fair dealing for the purpose of private study, research, criticism or review, no part of this publication may be reproduced, stored in a retrieval system, or transmitted in any form or by any means, electronic, electrical, chemical, mechanical, optical, photocopying, recording or otherwise, without the prior written permission of the copyright owner. Inquiries should be addressed to the Publishers

The right of T. H. Meyer to be identified as the author of this work has been asserted in accordance with sections 77 and 78 of the Copyright, Designs and Patents Act, 1988

A CIP catalogue record for this book is available from the British Library

ISBN 978 1 906999 94 0

Cover by Morgan Creative featuring photograph by T.H. Meyer
Typeset by DP Photosetting, Neath, West Glamorgan
Printed and bound by 4Edge Ltd., Essex

Contents

Author's Note vii

I

Departure 1
Syracuse 4
In the Greek Theatre 6
The Drive to Etna 8
Etna Speaks 12
Weininger Again 13
From Empedocles to Goethe's Faust 16
Conversation in a Sicilian Bower 18
A Dead-end Tourist Trail 21
Enna 22
Empedocles in Agrigento 24
Caltabelotta 25
Selinunte and Hecate 27
Klingsor 28
Farewell to Etna 29
Back in the Present 31
Turania 33
Farewell to Catania 34
Conversation on the Flight Home 34

II

Milazzo 45
Stromboli 49
The Workshop of Hephaestus 52

Palermo	54
Cagliostro, Goethe and Steiner	56
Parzival in Palermo	60
Phanuel and Enoch	60
Recent Earthquakes	65
Words Heard Within	67
Notes	69

Author's Note

This little book is probably the most—yet also paradoxically the least—personal of all my publications. Please disregard the title or the subtitle if it offends you.

It is written for anyone presently walking through burning lava who retains trust in the spiritual guidance given to human beings and humanity. The final sections were written during the period of terrible earthquakes in Nepal, which claimed the lives of ten thousand people.

Palermo, 29 April 2015

Those who strive towards the supersensible world seek at the same time to meet the Guardian of the Threshold. But doing so is not as easy as having a dreamlike imagination (...) Encountering this Guardian is a tragedy, a battle for survival involving all our knowledge, concepts, laws of cognition and our connection with the world of spirit, including with Ahriman and Lucifer. This catastrophe becomes inevitable if we wish to meet the Guardian of the Threshold.

Rudolf Steiner, 6 August 1918 (GA 181)[*]

We should not try to replace a true drama of cognition with a grammar of cognition, nor should fear prevent us lapsing into an individual abyss, for we rise from this again in association with many spirits, and experience our affinity with them. And thus we are born out of the world of spirit; but now we have absorbed and incorporated death, and even ourselves become a destroyer of what has come into being: we embody its spiritualization and are present at its destruction.

Rudolf Steiner, notebook (undated)

---

[*] *Dying Earth and Living Cosmos*, Rudolf Steiner Press 2015.

I

Departure

It was suddenly clear — I would go to Sicily. For a long time I had been involved in a project concerned with spiritual-scientific insights into the earth's interior.

And then a friend offered me his holiday house, a little north of Syracuse. His description of the place was alluring: peaceful, simple, off the beaten track, and a fine view; far away the Bay of Syracuse, and a strip of blue sea. It was tempting to think of carrying on my work in such surroundings.

A little later we were sitting in a street café in Basel. My friend had brought directions with him. From the rooftop, on a clear day, he said, you could see the peak of Etna on the horizon. The name Ludwig Polzer was mentioned; at the end of his life, unwontedly, he had gone to Italy alone. He visited Baia in the Bay of Naples — where, in his Roman incarnation as Hadrian, he had died in July of the year 138 — and climbed Vesuvius. Then he travelled on to Sicily, spending a few days in Taormina at the foot of Mount Etna.

We were about to pay when an unknown man at the next table shyly joined the conversation. He said he had read my biography of Polzer and had been touched by it. He had served for two years in the Swiss Guard in Rome. I looked at him enquiringly. 'Well,' I said, 'then you will have had some experience of the *Curia*, the Papal court.'

'Indeed I did,' he replied, rather hesitantly. 'Two years were enough.'

My interest in Etna arose as a kind of awakening from slumber. Since May, apparently, new seismic tremors had been reported in this region of Europe's biggest volcano, which becomes active at quite unpredictable intervals, spewing out fire and ash, and causing fatalities. Its victims meet the intransigent strength and power of Etna unprepared, sometimes while they're asleep at night. Unlike the enigmatic Empedocles, who hurled himself into its abyss around the middle of the fifth century BC, they do not willingly meet their end.

Early in the morning of 10 August 2014, I climbed aboard an Easyjet flight for Catania. As I got on, I was suddenly assailed by images of the disaster in Ukraine—not of the events at Maidan Square or the inferno in Odessa but of the Malaysian Airlines plane shot down over eastern Ukraine on 17 July. The poor unsuspecting victims! The whole world knows that the plane was shot down, but lies about who did it are assiduously spread by the western press. Since the events of 11 September 2001, the press, like a pack of trained dogs, has been hard at work attacking anything with the faintest whiff of 'conspiracy theory'.

In fact it was the quietest flight of my life. The steel bird flew calmly on its way, untroubled by the cloud banks it passed through. I couldn't tell whether we were flying over the Alps or not, and saw only a big, circular lake below, with a changing light playing on its surface. I immersed myself in the typescript I had brought with me: Rudolf Steiner's first lecture about the earth's interior, which he gave after the eruption of Vesuvius in April 1906. Right at the start of the lecture, Steiner stresses that it is much harder to investigate the interior of the earth than after-death states in kamaloka or the realm of devachan. But the Rosicrucians, he says, had undertaken such research, inspired in particular by Christian Rosenkreutz himself, who was able to do so as a purified Cain. Since Rosenkreutz was one of those who initiated Steiner, this research on the earth's interior can be also seen as a continuing task that his master assigned him.

*

Suddenly over the intercom comes the welcome announcement: 'Ladies and gentlemen, we are now flying over Rome towards Naples, and then on to Palermo.' Below us, on the horizon, Stromboli raises its smoking head from the waves—this little brother of Etna who outdoes the larger volcano with its almost uninterrupted outbursts. Then another announcement: 'We will soon be able to see Etna, which is emitting smoke at present. Passengers on the left side of the aircraft should certainly catch sight of it.' I was sitting on the left-hand side, alerted in advance to this possibility by my friend.

I laid the typescript to one side; and there it was. The mountain, a somewhat blunt pyramid resting on a broad pediment, appeared in the distance, sporting a clear plume of smoke that broadened and faded as it rose upwards. It was a sight both striking and exalted. Devout Buddhists may feel something like this when they catch their first glimpse of Fuji, Japan's sacred mountain, which is also a volcano and has a shape somewhat resembling that of Etna. Likewise, though in an experience still more intense, Laurence Oliphant was almost overwhelmed by the sight of the Himalayas when he was 22.

And so, uplifted by this view of Etna, I landed on the Island of Cain, as the anthroposophic historian Hans Gsänger once described Sicily. What a contrast to Ireland, which he called the Island of Abel.

Syracuse

Coming from Catania, it wasn't easy to find the cottage. I got help at a motorway service station, where two Carabinieri pointed me in the right direction. I was told to follow the road from Cassibile through Floridia. 'Floridia,' I repeated, and thanked them, at which one of the two men said in broken English, grinning under large mirrored sunshades: 'But not "Florida" in the USA!' It was as if he wished to say, 'We're already Americanized enough in Europe.'

I took a first evening stroll through the town, whose old town precinct Ortygia was overflowing with prosperous tourists seemingly oblivious to war—holidaymakers as every year. Rather than cars, a dense throng of pedestrians filled the whole main road. Unbothered by the crowd, as if the whole street belonged to him, an older man was making his way through the crush, carrying a giant CD player from which droned old Italian pop songs. They were meant to spread jollity perhaps. His gait was thoughtful, his deeply furrowed face profoundly earnest—like a fool from a Shakespeare play transported into modern times to personify a vacant cheeriness.

I walked past the cathedral. At its entrance stood a statue of St Paul—who, coming from Malta, passed through Syracuse on his way to Rome. Framing the portal were

Doric columns, which also support the aisles inside the building. They seemed literally to have stood still since the time of the temples to Athene.

The legendary Arethusa Spring embodies the connection between ancient Greece and Sicily. Pursued by a river god, the nymph Arethusa is said to have changed herself into a spring and, begging for the protection of the goddess Artemis (who also went under the byname of Ortygia), to have fled here through the Ionian Sea. By means of this metamorphosis she escaped a grievous destiny and brought a fount of Greek culture to Sicily.

Otto Weininger, a young intellectual, was drawn to this Arethusa Spring over a hundred years ago when he visited Syracuse in 1903. His revised dissertation 'Eros and Psyche' had just been brought out by the Viennese publisher Braumueller under the title *Geschlecht und Charakter (Sex and Character)*. Now, in Sicily, he feverishly awaited reactions to the book. 'I beg you,' he wrote to probably his closest friend Artur Geber, 'write to me very soon about *Sex and Character* and above all tell me what value you think the whole thing has...'[1]

*

In a side street, on my way back to the car which was parked in the Via Malta, I went into a small shop that sold CDs and guidebooks. Since the old, self-effacing shopkeeper was unable to take credit cards, I just asked him about performances in the Greek amphitheatre. 'All the big performances are over now,' he said with regret, and handed me the guidebook I had at first chosen. 'Take it! You can pay another time.' His wife gave me a brochure about the performances in Taormina. This simple gesture of unexpected kindness accompanied me as I made my way back through the noisy streets to my car.

In the Greek Theatre

There it lies, magnificent and harmoniously proportioned, in the dazzling heat. A couple of weeks back, Verdi's *Aida* was sung here. So many have sat here upon these steps, witnessing Greek tragedies with shock and dismay, or laughing at the jokes of Aristophanes...

Was Plato one of them? Sitting perhaps beside young Dion, his 'Antinous', who had summoned him to Syracuse? Unlike his beloved Dion, though, Plato could not persuade Dion's uncle Dionysius into the Platonic fold. Full of enthusiasm Plato came here three times, although he awoke the tyrant's anger on the first occasion so that the latter had him sold as a slave on his way home. An acquaintance had to buy back the 60-year-old's liberty for him. When Dion later took over rulership of the city, he developed tyrannical practices too, and was eventually murdered. After that, Plato relinquished any further efforts to put his political philosophy into practice. The failed experiment—similar to the one which Thomas à Becket would undertake in the twelfth century with the headstrong young King Henry II—showed him that the time for such ideas had not yet arrived. Plato's subsequent incarnations as the nun Rhoswitha in the tenth century, and the Goethe scholar Karl Julius Schröer, in the nineteenth century, were imbued with profoundly idealistic endeavour.[2] The reticence, or even wariness of this soul to realize ideas in outward deeds can perhaps be traced back to the karmic roots of this Sicilian venture.

Archimedes? He was born and died here. His grave lies near the theatre. An exhibition displays his discoveries and inventions including that of lever action. Archimedes is one of the few whose productive genius was celebrated in Rudolf Steiner's *Philosophy of Freedom*. Steiner describes thinking as the lever point of cognition that can lift the whole world off the mind's otherwise fixed hinges. Thinking itself, as Steiner found, is the most universal kind of leverage point which Archimedes sought in vain: 'Give me a place to stand and I will move the earth.' This self-sustaining point is found in the activity of thinking.

Archimedes studied and experimented day and night, though he will also presumably have relaxed a little at the comedies of Aristophanes. One day a Roman soldier walked into a circle he had drawn in the sand, and slew him when he objected. 'Do not intrude into my circles' were supposedly his last words.

And Aeschylus, the first of the great Greek tragedians? Surely he was present in this auditorium when his own plays were performed? Accused of betraying the mysteries, he escaped punishment by proving that he had not been initiated into any mysteries, although by birth he was connected with the Eleusian rites.

He travelled to Sicily on several occasions. In the year 480 BC he witnessed an eruption of Etna, as a couple of verses in *Prometheus Bound* testify. In Syracuse, according to a comment by Steiner, Aeschylus absorbed something of the impulse of dawning 'I' development. His Prometheus plays, of which only *Prometheus Bound* survives, bear witness to this spiritual intention. He died at Gela in Sicily.

Not far from the arena one finds the 'Ear of Dionysius', a remarkable, ear-shaped cave with notable acoustical properties. Perhaps Plato recited verses here with Dion, listening in delight to their multiple echoes. This picture of the two friends in the 'ear of Dionysius' is a striking one — as if the mere name of his young friend came to figure for Plato as a karmic memory, since, according to spiritual-scientific research, he himself subsequently incarnated as Dionysius the Younger.

All this still seems to linger in the etheric atmosphere of the city: a dionysian-luciferic spirituality, transplanted here from Greece as an inspiration for science and art.

*

A walk to Ortygia, the old heart of Syracuse, concluded my visit to the city on this occasion. Today swans were swimming in the small pond fed by the Arethusa Spring.

I looked for the old shopkeeper but only found his wife there. Surprised, she took what I owed. No doubt she hadn't expected I would return. On my way back to the car, the 'Fool' with his music machine came into view again, walking slowly and deliberately, and with the same earnest expression as the day before. In the city where world theatre of such magnificence has been performed, he too gives his own small performance each night.

The Drive to Etna

But now Etna — whose smoking plume had already greeted me from afar when I was in the plane — was calling to me.

Not far from Catania I had a closer view of the smouldering smokestack. The height and shape of the dark swathe of fumes kept changing all the time. You could see that the mountain was a *living being*.

In Nicolosi I visited an excursion agency to ask about a cable car trip to the crater region. This would not take me all the way to the summit because of the low-level eruptions at the crater. The last bit, they said, would be done in a large jeep, with a guide. The lady at the ticket counter urged me to go now, today: 'Don't postpone it until tomorrow! Who knows how things will be then.' I wouldn't be able to go to the 'Philosopher's Tower' therefore, in which Empedocles had stayed before he threw himself into the depths of the crater. I comforted myself with the thought that in May 1787 even Goethe, who had also taken a draughtsman with him, was prevented by bad weather from getting any further than Nicolosi.

After a few minutes the cable car was sliding silently up the side of the mountain, over giant fields of cold lava that testified to previous great eruptions. Suddenly, below me, I saw wonderful islands of colour: vivid yellow in the rust-brown lava field — *Senecio glauco* (ragwort), indigenous to Etna, then Etna broom — and pink cushions of Sicilian soapwort. At about 2000 metres we had to climb aboard the jeep, which carried around 20 people and drove us to the south flank. My first impression after getting out was of successive thunderous detonations and columns of smoke shooting abruptly heavenwards. Suddenly the mountain had a *voice*!

From closer at hand you could see that the pillars of smoke rising like fountains were repeatedly mingled with red; and from time to time 'pyroclastic material', as science calls it, erupted. More commonly known as 'bombs', these ejecta were hurled upwards and outwards with huge momentum and then, seemingly slowly, almost in time lapse tempo, fell back through the air. Standing there one felt exposed to the mountain's strength and destructive power.

Involuntarily, other images came to me as I watched — of the destruction of the Twin Towers in New York in September 2001. Photos of that event published later show very similar smoke fountains gathering into upward soaring and coiling plumes, which bore within them parts of the buildings such as iron girders. Like the lava bombs these were hurled upwards and sideways, then seemed to sink back slowly. Anyone who has ever witnessed even a moderate volcanic eruption will *know* that the New York towers were not destroyed by *two aeroplanes*. This mainstay of the official account had never seemed so ridiculous to me as it did now that afternoon on Etna. And I had to ask this: were subterranean powers, as they manifest in even a minor natural eruption, not also at work in those dire events of 2001?

Returning to the jeep after several hours, I asked the driver whether any lava flow might be visible. 'Oh yes, especially at night. But to see it you'd have to go to the north side, to Fornazza.' In Fornazza I was told to visit Cicelli, which lies a little higher up the slope.

The mountain café and the parking place in front of it were heaving with visitors eager to see the spectacle. Cars were parked in almost every available space. As I drank a cappucino and looked out at the peak of the new subcrater on the north side of the mountain, a red dot became visible around twilight, and became ever more pronounced. German words filled my ears — apparently accurate explanations of the unfolding drama. After a while I joined the discussion with my own questions. I learned that the new crater had been more or less active for months now, and that lava was erupting from its lateral vent at a temperature of around 1200 degrees Celsius.

And where does it come from? An older gentleman told me: 'From vast depths of the earth's interior. We know scarcely anything about them, except at most that the core of the earth is said to consist of iron and nickel. But this too is only a scientific theory of course. One remarkable fact is the parallel discovered between eruptions of Stromboli and Etna. They might be connected by subterranean channels in the earth's interior. Who knows. It's all mysterious.' I thought about introducing something from 'spiritual-scientific theory' as well; but, apart from a reference to the nine strata of the earth's interior as Dante speaks of them, I decided against it. The group, whose leader I had addressed, was keen to head off now and view from a better vantage point the colourful spectacle that would soon become visible as night fell. 'Go back to Fornazza,' they said. Out in the open there you're at a further distance, but you have a better overview of everything.'

From there the red dot revealed itself to be the source of a lava stream flowing in two channels many kilometers downwards. The darkness brought it to light. Above this was the stack of the new crater, with continual detonations, both weaker and stronger, and ascending fountains of dark and lighter smoke shot through with red. There was a restless, unpredictable flickering of light above, and below it the ever-shining red source of the lava flow, which ran in two streams to begin with, only to merge into one further down. It looked like a brindled snake. A picture that came to me was the suddenly luminous snake in Goethe's Fairy Tale. It creates the bridge that connects two worlds: that of the senses and that of the spirit. And one day it will help unite the scientific explanations of such extraordinary natural phenomena with the insights of spiritual science. Today they still stand disconnected next to each other, as, on this evening, the views of the kind gentleman and the author's unexpressed intention.

Etna Speaks

It is one thing to know a spiritual-scientific insight in theory, quite another to experience it in situ. Here it was possible to *feel* the fathomless connection between the human being and the earth, between microcosm and macrocosm. Etna speaks, talks to us. Its alphabet is composed of detonation, fiery eruption, glowing lava, earth tremors. In this, its language, it says:

> O man, what you hear and see here, which often awakens your fear or terror, which can destroy life and yet in turn make the earth fertile again—none of this would be if you did not continually cause uproar in my depths with your unpurified emotions. I am rooted in the macrocosmic counterpart, in the earth's depths, of your tumultuous passions. My roots extend down into the sixth stratum, the fire earth. When this stratum is thrown into upheaval through you, the fire-earth soul pushes through channels into the upper strata and thence into the upper world in which your outward body exists. And here everything of me you now experience is made manifest as earthquake or fire

activity. Your soul body is one with the earth's depths. Purify it, and then I too one day will be cleansed and will grow tranquil. Strive like Francis of Assisi who once kindled before me the fire of deepest soul striving. O man, do not forget that you are not separate from the world, that you are a unity with her and all her elements. The great Empedocles already knew this when he hurled himself into me and so united with me. So *cast your spirit* into me; and from this fall you can also draw the strength for an ascent. O man, hear my speech: redeem yourself — and me.

Weininger Again

How differently Otto Weininger experienced Etna in the summer of 1903!

He wrote to Artur Geber on 3 August 1903: 'Etna struck me most by the imposing *shamelessness* of its crater. A crater is reminiscent of the backside of a mandrill.' Though this is not particularly tasteful, Weininger nevertheless has a sense of the *soul quality* connected with a volcano. He uses the ethical concept of shamelessness, and associates the volcano with the manifestation of something subhuman. His imagination is certainly remarkable. We can also easily surmise what he would have done with the mandrill metaphor if he had seen Etna smoking and spewing fire!

From a spiritual perspective, things look different: we need courage and absolutely truthful self-scrutiny when we examine our own subhuman qualities. Faced with them we might wish the 'ground would swallow us up' for shame. It is our human shamelessness that ought by rights to be associated with anything volcanic in nature, especially when the fire earth begins to spew forth its innards.

*

Otto Weininger is one of the most interesting subjects of Rudolf Steiner's karmic enquiries. His trip to southern Italy and Sicily in the summer of 1903 was also a journey to the scenes of his former incarnation. Tommaso Campanella languished in Neapolitan dungeons for 27 years. His life as Weininger in a sense made up for this lost time. Thus, after working through most of his 'lost time', in the autumn of 1903 this task was suddenly complete—there was nothing more to make good. And now he should have taken up something *entirely new*. But he met a void and could not discover what this new thing should be. And so Weininger no longer waited for all the turbulent responses to his magnum opus, but instead, renting the house in Vienna where Beethoven died, he shot himself in the chest on 4 October 1903 at the age of 23. He did so, as August Strindberg wrote to Artur Gerber, by 'permission of the loftiest source, for otherwise such a thing does not occur.'

According to Steiner's research, Otto Weininger had brought with him a soul foundation of substantial spiritual quality.[3] He underwent a Jewish incarnation as a woman, in the period of the Babylonian Captivity. This woman had powerful clairvoyant and visionary gifts. Then, after a male incarnation in the early post-Christian era, much of these ancient impulses resurfaced in the visionary and revolutionary deeds of Tommaso Campanella, who rebelled against the dominion of Spain in southern Italy and paid for this insurgency with torture and imprisonment. In this period of incarceration, the old spirituality in his being in a sense became blocked. And more than this, the soul of Campanella after death found that the incarceration it had suffered was actually *in opposition* to this keen spirituality, and *caused* by its incarnation as a Jewish woman. Dr Otto Weininger's former spirituality was irreconcilable with his academic intellectualism at the turn of the twentieth century. Yet this subjective spiritual element, now become problematic, continued to linger within a soul housed in a body which, on his mother's side, also had Hungarian-Turanian elements.

The spiritual element, which the soul itself opposed, metamorphosed in its incarnation as Weininger into a double hatred: for the feminine principle (not women as such) and for the Jewish race (but not individual Jews). Thus his book *Sex and Character* is the *karmic autobiography* of a soul who had to live out conflicting impulses carried over from previous incarnations. Only detailed karma vision could have given this inner conflict a different direction and outcome. It is no accident that Strindberg felt so close to Weininger. His anti-female sentiments were due to a very similar opposition towards one of his own former incarnations as a woman.[4]

Thus Weininger's self-chosen demise can also be seen as an intentional fall into volcanic abysses of the soul, of which vulcanism offers us an *outward* picture. A few months after he visited Etna, Otto Weininger threw himself into an *inner* Etna. On the day of his suicide he admitted to his friend Gerber: 'I know that I am a born criminal, a born murderer.' Ultimately he killed himself to make sure he didn't murder others. It was Weininger's noble error that he failed to see that *all people*, not just him, bear within them the potential seed of all kinds of criminality. This is the subhuman, volcanic nature that resides in everyone and, as in Weininger's case, sometimes erupts.

Confrontation with the subhuman within us is something people will increasingly have to experience. Conventional ethical norms will gradually become less and less capable of suppressing this, as is apparent if we observe our own times and the flagrant evil that rears its head everywhere. It is to be hoped that ever more people will learn to meet and survive the dramatic conflict with evil *within them*, in a grounded loyalty to and perception of the spirit, thus developing a higher, truer power of goodness. All evil, in fact, is the manure that nurtures the development of a higher good.

But let's return to Empedocles, of whom Etna spoke and still speaks, and who ultimately united himself with it in a most mysterious way.

From Empedocles to Goethe's Faust

This is what history tells us: Empedocles, the Greek natural philosopher, mystic and priest at the temple of Agrigento, threw himself into Etna around 430 BC. The Philosophers' Tower where he dwelt beforehand is at present buried under a new lava flow. Some academics think the story of his unusual death is a legend, and they regard Empedocles only as the originator of the doctrine of the four elements. Steiner's occult research led him to deeper insights: Empedocles was one of those who prepared a new I consciousnesss that would place the human being entirely on his own footing. This resembled Aeschylus' endeavours in a different domain, primarily in his Prometheus plays.

Steiner speaks of the self-sacrifice of Empedocles: he gave up his supersensible bodies to the elements in order to lend an even greater power of indestructibility to the growing I impulse.

This deed of Empedocles imbued the etheric atmosphere of Sicily.

Steiner's karma research also pursued the path of this immortal individuality in creating a new personality body—as Georg Faust, the alchemist, magician and mystic who died in Staufen around 1541. Like Luther he wrestled with the devil. Overcoming death by a new incarnation, he embarked on the approaching task of the era, the engagement and battle with evil.

The legend of Faust was based on Georg Faustus, and in his own day Goethe picked up this thread.

Various traits of Faust in Part I of Goethe's play can be seen as the elaboration of actual characteristics belonging to this figure of Georg Faustus: the scene, for instance, where Faust invokes the elements and enters into connection with the spirit of the earth. And the whole of Goethe's play is, surely, the purest embodiment of the I principle, of unceasing spiritual striving—one which also necessarily calls forth the adversary powers, represented by Goethe in the figure of Mephisto. These powers are the same that in Sicily were embodied and focused in the figure of Klingsor.

And the Mothers in Part II of *Faust*—they too point towards Sicily, which especially also counts mother godesses amongst its divinities. A passage in Plutarch drew Goethe's attention to the cult of mother godesses in Engyon, Sicily, a colony of Crete in the province of Enna in the seventh century BC. Thus Goethe's trip to Sicily was valuable not only for his discovery of the archetypal plant—we can recall his experience in the botanical gardens at Palermo — but also for his poetic elaboration of *Faust*.

That Goethe himself did not reach the peak of Etna, and therefore did not see the place of Empedocles' sacrifice with his own eyes, may have helped kindle his striving for true I development still more strongly.

Conversation in a Sicilian Bower

'You see, if you wish to understand Sicily you have to understand Empedocles,' said the older gentleman whom I had never set eyes on until a day ago. His eyes shone behind his glasses. Sparse grey hair, sticking out on both sides, made him look like a philosopher.

'He was a priest at Agrigento, and must have suffered unspeakably to see how human beings were increasingly shut out from the world of the higher gods.'

His wife brought out a drink of almond milk on a tray to the cool garden bower. I tasted it, and was reminded of marzipan, which I used to like so much as a child.

'He could have just given up the struggle as others did. He didn't. He saw that the path to the spirit henceforth leads through the darkness of matter. Yet whether or not someone embarks on this new path remains his own free, earthly deed. The gods no longer guide us. And here in the darkness lurk all the powers of Klingsor, ready to seize hold of the human being who has been discharged from the hands of the gods, and befuddle him over his deeper destiny. Empedocles overcame fear and united with the earthly depths. He trusted in the bright, warm I at his centre.'

Conversation in a Sicilian Bower 19

'As did Hieram,' I interjected, 'who likewise threw himself into the fire, and embarked on the journey to the centre of the earth.'

'Yes, Hieram and Empedocles pursue the same path,' confirmed my philosopher.

'Hieram's goal,' I went on, 'was to discover Cain at the centre of the earth — but in the condition in which he was before the lapse into primal discord. This Cain was the one Hieram sought. The *ur*-Cain, and at the same time the new one.'

'And so Empedocles, in his own way, also entered the realm of the original Cain,' said the philosopher. 'All spirit henceforth must be found anew out of the inner spark of the I. The ancient divine light of the gods, endowed from without, has been once and for all extinguished.'

'Sicily is also called the Island of Cain,' I said. 'But which Cain does this refer to?'

'A good question, a good question,' said the philosopher with a smile, which showed that he preferred new enigmas to fixed conclusions. After a pause he added: 'Let us put it like this. If the human I does not, as Hieram did, penetrate to the centre of the earth, since prevented from doing so by the Klingsor powers, then it remains only an image of the *fallen* Cain. In so far as Sicily is subject to the dominion of the power of Klingsor, it is indeed the land of the *old* Cain.

'The Mafia, the power of the Church and so forth?' I asked.

'Oh those are only the outermost dross,' said the philosopher. 'It is worth noting, however, that US governments, which are so obsessed with power, have always made use of the mafioso element in Sicily.'

'The path to the spirit,' I continued, 'thus passes through

the earth's interior at whose centre the paradisiacal Cain waits to be awoken by us — if we can put it like that. Thus Empedocles pursued the path to the Cain who was, at the same time, both primordially ancient and new. Surely all who dare follow in the footsteps of Empedocles make Sicily into a land of the *positive* primordial Cain?'

'We can regard it like that,' said the philosopher. 'You see, everything depends on whether we grasp the I-spark and, with its growing light of thinking, seek to illumine and encompass the spirit. And this spark can only be kindled in the darkest depths of the earth. This is also the true mission of central Europeans such as Goethe, Fichte, Hegel and Steiner.'

'Apropos of Fichte,' I remarked, 'he seems to have had an intimation of the polarity between the I and the earth's depths, the latter of course the source of the lava flows.'

'Tell me more,' said the philosopher eagerly.

'Well, Fichte once said that most people would be more likely to think of themselves as a lump of *lava* from the moon than as an I!'

'Astonishing! So in his own way he clearly knew that the I must be wrested from the earth's depths, otherwise it will lose itself to a lava-type counter-I, which the Klingsor powers can seize and employ.'

His wife cleared the drinks away, and mentioned in passing that it seemed to her that her soul, like that of her husband, had a central European quality which had been transplanted to Sicily — almost so as to perish here.

'Only if we perish can we be reborn,' said the philosopher in a tone simultaneously knowing and admonishing. 'After all, Christ descended into the depths of the earth after death, before his resurrection.'

'Empedocles as forerunner of Christ's deed?' I asked.

'Let us say, he followed the path of Christ before Christ himself, as, after Christ's time, did Francis of Assisi, Fichte, Hegel and Goethe, each in their own way; and Steiner of course.' Then, after a pause, he added: 'In fact, when Goethe came here from Italy he said: "Sicily is the key to everything." He was right. And the key to this key is Empedocles.'

*

I spent the evening in the Greek theatre at Taormina, where Beethoven's first piano concerto was performed. One can't imagine a lovelier setting for this Promethean music of the modern era! At the end, the orchestra played the prelude to Wagner's *Tristan*, strangely appropriate here where one can look out over the sea. Suddenly, after dark had fallen, I became aware that the narrow red column of lava had interposed itself between two Greek columns.

A Dead-end Tourist Trail

'If you drive to Enna, don't forget to visit the Lake of Pergusa,' the philosopher had told me as we took our leave of each other. 'Here, according to ancient tradition, Persephone was stolen by Pluto.'

Persephone is the human soul that lost the power of clairvoyance — succumbing to the earth's intrinsic forces as embodied by Pluto. This is the loss of which Empedocles complained, but then accepted, dying in a way that heralded the new, earth-born powers of clairvoyance.

In his lovely book about Sicily, Hans Gsänger gives a

vivid account of the connection between Enna, its lake nearby, and the legend of Persephone, which seems primarily to unfold in Eleusis, where Edouard Schuré also set his Eleusian plays. But Sicily, in its strong affinity with the earth—whereas Greece lived from the *sea*—was strongly opposed to all clairvoyance; and therefore the legend, drawn from ancient vision, places the birth of Persephone's mother Demeter in Enna, and the death of her daughter Persephone at Lake Pergusa.

Whereas Gsänger paints poetic and atmospheric pictures of Lake Pergusa with its groves of eucalyptus, the modern visitor is inevitably disappointed. The small, oval lake is encircled by a car racing track which interposes itself between the lake and the visitor, and hides it from view behind impenetrable fences. Once the lake, and the idyllic and earnest atmosphere emanating from it, reminded the visitor of the loss of ancient clairvoyance. Today, technological powers drawn from the earth's depths have robbed it of this last picture, and of the least sense of the clairvoyance killed off by Pluto's earthly forces.

Enna

A different symptom, from a later date, of Enna's connection with the thorough demise of ancient clairvoyance is the baroque style of the cathedral's columns. They bear Corinthian capitals, from one of which a ghastly head of Medusa gazes down upon the visitor. Hellish monsters surround its pediment. The clairvoyance stolen by Pluto had already sunk to the state of perceiving only the dregs of the spiritual astral world. Perseus did not steal this decadent clairvoyance, but pointed instead to the way to transform it into *powers of thinking*.

Of the ancient shrine to Ceres and Demeter there is nothing left in Enna but a large lump of stone, on a ledge in the rockface that offers a far view towards Etna. Gsänger is right to emphasize that Pergusa and this high rock shrine belong together as do Persephone and Demeter, the latter often of course depicted bearing an ear of corn. Demeter surveying the granary of Sicily! Instead of ancient clairvoyance, a spiritualization of the earth: perhaps anthroposophy will best be realized in this island through a new form of agriculture.

Waldorf schools? Just a single one, in Palermo. Inner resistance to a new spirituality is apparent here.

*

Enna has always been a contested place, but hard to conquer. A few steps from the Demeter cliff stands the massive fortress which Frederick II of the Staufer dynasty was especially proud of. Another Frederick II—from Aragonia—had a tower built here. Though it was opening time, there was no attendant to be seen anywhere.

An old gentleman, who was walking his dog on the meadow around the tower, addressed me kindly. He was an engineer, a road-builder. Now he likes travelling a lot: in Vietnam, Egypt, Greece. He has been to Switzerland too. Where did he still intend visiting? 'Kazakhstan,' he said. We mention Ukraine. 'Hopefully there won't be a Third World War,' said the engineer. 'It's on the cards,' I replied, caused, as we agree, by the hunt for resources and geopolitical conflict. We set off to find the absent attendant. 'The immigrants,' continues the engineer as we walk.

'Lampedusa is bursting with them. Malta doesn't let any in.' That's strange, I think: the place where St Paul worked, and later the Templars and the Order of Malta.

We find *her* at last, the attendant, at the car park. But before I go to see the tower, the engineer invites me to the café. People there greet him—they know him. He is respected. He reminds me that Enna was not only the spiritual navel of Sicily but, at the time Syracuse became a world metropolis, also the centre of the whole western world. I wish him many happy trips across the world, and he wishes me a good journey.

Enna, the former heart of this island, also reminds us that, despite being surrounded by ocean, Sicily never became a seafaring nation—unlike Carthage, Rome, Greece, Portugal, England, Holland and even Venice.

*

As I was eating an evening meal of risotto in Caltanisetta, the innkeeper, who had worked in Dusseldorf for many years, said there wasn't really much to see there. I contradicted him, praising the pleasant, easygoing atmosphere in the main street, full of young and old—which apparently even Goethe enjoyed when he once visited.

'If you really want a pleasant sight,' he insisted, 'go to the Piazza Armerina. There you'll find vivid scenes depicted on some wonderful mosaics, unique in Sicily.' I promised to do so.

Empedocles in Agrigento

A walk through the temple area of Agrigento, which the Greek colonists called Akraga. The 'Porto di Empedocle' offers a purely outward reminder of the great philosopher who lived and taught here. Having turned down a government appointment that was offered to him, he wandered through the land as a healer, physician and magician. But here in Agrigento he was, above all, a temple priest. Did he hold office in the very well preserved temple, visible from afar, that stands on, or rather dominates, a small peninsula? From far away, without the intruding sight of people, its impression is most striking. It was a house of God that only priests might enter. Just as the gods lived in their temples, so they lived also in the breast of the high priest. With his god in his heart, Empedocles ended his influential life when he threw himself into far-off Etna. This too was divine service.

Caltabelotta

Soon after Agrigento, a first signpost to Caltabelotta informs us it is 66 kilometres away. This number becomes emblematic of our further journey: driving through a sparse landscape, with little traffic, in the burning midday heat. Far away on a range of cliffs, as if glued to them, a village comes into view. Overhung by a steep rockface, this must be the place where Klingsor unfolded his destructive power and directed it at the western world. Still today this power gleams like Etna does, even if apparent only to inner apprehension.

The village before Caltabelotta, the actual site of Klingsor's dominion, takes our car in steep zig-zags through narrow, winding streets. The surrounding landscape appears dead, deeply grave. It is hard to imagine children's laughter not being immediately suffocated here.

Arriving in Caltabelotta, the whole atmosphere is heavy as lead. I go up the tor where Klingsor kept watch for any knight of the Holy Grail approaching who might perhaps be tempted and succumb to him. I have to admit that I had to force myself to stand here. I remembered friends who had been here before me. I wanted to know what they *must* have felt in this place. There is something objective in the atmosphere here that reaches far beyond one's merely personal mood.

I reflected on the fact that Lord Stanhope, who later tempted and corrupted Kaspar Hauser, had suffered several days of unconsciousness in *Sicily* in the year Hauser was born. Did this represent an influx into him of a power that henceforth governed him? And Alistair Crowley, who played carelessly with the profoundest realities like an adolescent, who declared himself a god, spread his maleficent seed in *Sicily*. Then there was Charles Leadbeater who chose a hotel suite in Taormina as the place to conduct the second initiation of his own 'Kaspar Hauser', who went by the name of Krishnamurti.

The steps were narrow and steep. After a while an iron handrail offered me support.

Every step was arduous. And strangely, it felt as if time itself held its breath. Steps with no progress. The very reverse of what Parzival experienced when he climbed to the Grail Castle by the side of Gurnemanz. He scarcely feels the feet that bear him upwards but is, rather, lifted aloft by the noble goal. How different this experience: even my feet felt leaden.

And although I ascend, after a while it seems as if every step leads downwards into the depths. The earth's interior seems to become immanent, especially that stratum of it that Dante calls the Cain layer. This is the deep locus in the earth that inspires all human discord. This layer of discord seems to rise up like vapour towards you. And reaching the summit — or, in one's inner experience, the nadir — it is crowned by the sphere formed of the very substance of evil, the source and fount of the blackest magic on earth. Here only one thought keeps us standing: that the strongest evil originates in a much stronger, sublime good — not in order that we succumb to it, but to engender a great good through our own resources.

Can one 'enjoy' this prospect of the reversal of high and low? Anyone who still aspires to the noble ideals of human endeavour will want to get away from here as fast as possible! Before we can transform and redeem such evil — which we must eventually do in a far distant future — we will first have to become better than we are (much, much better).

As I descended again, I was reminded of a similar ascent I had made many years ago at Adam's Peak in Sri Lanka, the holy mountain revered by Muslims and Buddhists alike. I'm sure it was higher than this tor and the ascent took longer. But everything was so different. It is said that Adam first set foot on solid ground there after his blameless fall from Paradise. On special festival days a giant footprint in the rock is uncovered. Getting to the top was a great exertion, and the panoramic view a gift. And never before, perhaps, have I found an ordinary Ceylon tea, handed me by a monk, so welcome and tasty.

Selinunte and Hecate

In Selinunte, again, there is a well-preserved temple standing alone in the landscape. Through its columns shimmers the blue of the ocean. This was an extensive site, built directly by the sea, with a temple of Zeus and Hera before it and a mighty acropolis. And outside the old town, beyond a river, one finds the sacred precincts of Demeter, and the mysterious Hecate. The very fact that she is called the 'threefold one' indicates her enigmatic nature. She was regarded as a divinity of the dead, but she also had the power to change one life form into another, and it seems this corresponds more to her being. What must necessarily have happened to the human body, soul and spirit after Persephone, the old power of clairvoyance, had vanished from them? Or to put it another way: what forces must the etheric body itself weave henceforth to be able to penetrate the physical body, the etheric body itself and astral body? Hecate gave a threefold answer to this question. Goethe knew the secret of Hecate, which figures in Part II of *Faust*. But without Steiner's illumination, these passages remain very difficult to comprehend.[5]

Hecate is connected with continuous change, as manifest to us in the ocean's waves. She was called the 'Goddess of Transformations'. Water is her element, just as that of Klingsor is stone that lapses from all growth and development, becoming dead and extinct — lava without fertility.

Klingsor

Thus what occurred in Enna and Pergusa continued in Selinunte. After the loss of clairvoyance, the etheric body had to be completely transformed so as to adapt it to the sensory knowledge that was prepared at the time, but also to the new spiritual knowledge of the future. Hecate stands in the service of humanity's evolution. Klingsor is her adversary, since he hates all deeper evolution. Mafia and Church, like all other anti-developmental streams of humanity, are therefore generally subject to his sway.

Hans Gsänger had a sure sense of things when he drew attention to the strange position occupied by Caltabelotta in the etheric geography of Italy, and indeed of all Europe and the Near East. Selinunte, Caltabelotta and Enna lie on the same line; and if we extend the sightline from Caltabelotta to Syracuse across the sea, we come to Alexandria. Then finally, drawing a line from Caltabelotta through Palermo, we reach Capua, near Naples. Gsänger summarizes all this as follows:

> Like a spider Klingsor sat in the web of various decisive streams that he sought to influence from Caltabelotta. As in human beings themselves, good and evil lived close alongside each other in the Sicilian landscape. The lords of Caltabelotta sought to steal the parts of man's nature that had slipped beyond his grasp since the loss of the old clairvoyance.[6]

But in Sicily there was also a mystery site where initiates cultivated a knowledge of the processes in the human body that were connected with this loss of the old clairvoyance. These secrets were preserved in the temple of Hecate in Selinunte.[7]

Farewell to Etna

My return journey followed the Palermo ring road. I hadn't seen this city for more than 40 years, and then only for a few hours when my ship from Tunis docked here. Vague, dark memories surfaced nebulously within me. Were they to be reawoken, refreshed and complemented with new impressions? What, I heard friends asking in perplexity, you didn't visit Monreale with its unique mosaics, the botanical gardens or the cathedral? Indeed I didn't. I left Palermo where it lay. It was Etna that was calling me, not Palermo. One can know that Goethe made the great botanical discovery of his Italian trip in the gardens at Palermo, when he had an inner vision of the archetypal plant, without having to suffer the noise and heat of the crowded streets. In passing, we can also recall that in 1910 Steiner brought the glad message of the new Christ event here. We don't need to leave the ring road, either, to imagine that he too most probably endowed the etheric atmosphere of Sicily with a new quality when he stayed here—a subtler one perhaps than that of Empedocles and Klingsor, but no less persistent in its influence...

And yet I'm worried that the sight of the exit signpost to 'Monreale' will weaken my resolve, and tempt me to go there after all. Luckily no such signpost appeared, and I drove on. The art of travel sometimes simply involves not seeing signposts... or not heeding them. I'd done this back in Agrigento too, where there were many waymarkers to Luigi Pirandello's birthplace. How fine a thing it would have been to learn more about this mysterious author, who chose this of all places for his latest incarnation.

But the strongest argument of all for not leaving the ring road round Palermo was this. Hadn't I made Etna a kind of promise? Hadn't I promised to return, and take my leave of it, though only if my travels had inwardly enriched me? They had, even if some of my impressions were still proving hard to assimilate. I dared only meet Etna face-to-face if I was changed on my return, albeit only to the smallest degree. I must come back as someone who was in some way altered. Anything else would not have been *travelling* but merely moving on from one place to another.

*

I would be flying back tomorrow. I wasted no time but drove towards Catania. As I drove, the mountain of enigmas, which can be seen from a long way off in good weather, remained shrouded in mist. I soon reached Nicolosi, from where I had set off a week before. There he stood before me again, without smoke or fire. The atmosphere was calm. I entered the same Etna tour agency again, just before it shut. The same lady who had urged me so insistently to ascend immediately now declared, 'It's all over. For the time being of course. He's been quiet for a couple of days now.' His tranquillity became mine. I was dismissed.

I could set off for home.

Back in the Present

At the hotel I cast my eye over the *Repubblica* newspaper. Suddenly my attention was caught by news that ISIS Jihadists originally cultivated by the US had posted on the net a video, with commentary, of the execution of a US journalist. Then, on the TV, I saw horrendous images from the Near East, and from Ukraine.

Yes, Klingsor-Cain is continuing to spread the poison of discord and conflict. In homoeopathic dosage this pervades all the symptoms of decline and degeneracy in our time. It also acts as an anaesthetic to *dull* us to the present workings of Ahriman. Klingsor-Cain acts as a shield or screen behind which Ahriman, in his first and last incarnation, is set to act with as little hindrance as possible. What most effectively hinders Ahriman? Spiritual-scientific awareness of him: the knowledge that his incarnation is happening *now*. 'The mystic light on earth is burning me,' says Ahriman in Scene 12 of Steiner's mystery play *The Soul's Awakening*. Yet who are the souls who really wish to awaken? Certainly not those who take, or reject, such words as mere 'poetry'. The shield with which Klingsor protects Ahriman is forged from all kinds of human weaknesses: the love of comfort, a materialistic outlook, all kinds of egotisms, fear—above all fear of truth and knowledge, and also fear of falling into the 'abyss of individuality'. Klingsor's spear is hatred for the higher gods and for all true spirituality in the world.

But here at the foot of Mount Etna it should not be forgotten that the lower Cain can be vanquished, in the same way that Hieram raised—or we can also say—deepened—and purified the fallen Cain within him. Just as all earth evolution culminates in the Vulcan condition, so in all lower Cain-Klingsor nature there lives the seed for a new condition in which we can rise to an archetypal innocence again, but now out of our own intrinsic strength. That is the deeper meaning of the connection between the names 'Cain' and 'Vulcan', the latter the term given to earth's highest evolutionary stage.

*

Just saw a 'Cross Talk' on the internet: a new one at last from Peter Lavelle on the RT Moscow news channel: 'Why is Putin so *demonized* by the western media?' The word is used repeatedly, but a real, spiritual dimension is lacking. The word 'demon' is used as an empty term. In Dante it was far more tangible. He places traitors in the eighth circle of hell, the 'Cain layer' — corresponding to the eighth layer of the earth's interior. The soul of someone who betrays others, says Dante, is devoured by the demon of betrayal and must live in the depths of the earth, even if his body still lives above on the earth's surface, sundered from the soul. Such betrayal of the truth is flagrant and ubiquitous today, and includes the betrayal of anthroposphical substance.

Turania

A night of turbulence and dream images. I'm in conversation with a politician and impress on him the strange fact that Sicily so far has only one Waldorf school whereas 25 have been established in Hungary since 1989.

Hungary too has volcanic activity, and its folk soul has a Turanian strain. Atlantis went under due to betrayal of the Vulcan mysteries during the *ancient Turanian* epoch. The mission of Hungary is: to refine the Turanian element.

The Count of St Germain was born in Hungary, as were Rudolf Steiner and other great sons of Cain and leading spirits. Thence they drew their impetus to aspire to the loftiest heights. In Hungary some have embarked on the path from fallen Cain to primordial Cain. Secrets of etheric geography: Hungary could become exemplary for Sicily. But *here* the path to the primordial Cain must no doubt pass through a new fertility of the earth. Demeter — agriculture.

Farewell to Catania

A last tour of Catania. At the hotel entrance there's a colourful handwritten notice: 'Etna Sunset — only 45 euros'. And in small script below it: 'minimum 3 people'. The lady at reception clarifies, 'Only if there is anything worth seeing'. The offer is unlikely to be taken up before the next Etna eruption.

Just inside the cathedral there's a monument to Bellini, who was born here. Notes from his opera *Norma* have been chiselled into the stone.

Outside in the square is the famous monument with the elephant rising from a fountain. On the fountain itself are inscribed verses from Ovid's *Metamorphoses*. I am again reminded of Sri Lanka where Ovid, in his later incarnation as Laurence Oliphant, climbed Adam's Peak, the mountain on which Adam first set foot on terra firma. This was at the end of the Lemurian period — the time of fishes or Pisces. A catastrophic fire unleashed by unbridled human passions caused the downfall of this ancient continent. Strange to reflect on this fact at the foot of Mount Etna. Since that time humanity has passed through a cosmic year into the *modern* Piscean age: a Platonic year of 26,000 years during which the gods have worked for millennia on the human *body and soul*. For some centuries now we have been in the Piscean age once more, but now at a higher level — or at least *potentially* so.

Conversation on the Flight Home

I had booked a window seat in the right aisle and arrived in good time at Catania airport. Soon after the flight took off, I

Conversation on the Flight Home 35

peered through the small oval window towards the mountain of miracles. There he was again, greeting me with his whitish-grey plume of smoke, as soundlessly as on the flight here.

Shortly before we took off I had glanced briefly at the passenger who sat next to me but taken no further notice of him – a gentleman of dark complexion and black hair, in his early forties. Now he leaned towards me, and spoke to me in a pleasant, sonorous voice, with interest apparent in his gentle yet wakeful eyes.

'Your first trip to Sicily?' he asked.

'Yes and no,' I said.

'Yes *and* no?' he repeated.

'Yes. You see, I did cross the country once, from Palermo to Messina – over 40 years ago. But back then I was only looking with my eyes. My soul was still asleep, if I can put it like that.'

'And now you have been travelling with a wakened soul?'

'More awake than before, at any rate. You should never think that you can't be still more awake...'

The man smiled and nodded silently. 'Yes, there are many degrees of wakefulness,' he said with confidence and a mysterious undertone in his voice.

'And so Etna drew you, did it?' he went on, more in confirmation than question.

'Yes, that's right,' I said, somewhat astonished. 'It just so happened that I arrived at Etna at the right moment – as it became active.'

'Yes,' he said, 'at the right moment. Sometimes things work out in a remarkable way, don't they?' And after a short pause he added: 'What a wonderful opportunity to glimpse nature's secrets – and those of the human soul.'

'Certainly it was a magnificent experience. Yet science seems to have little to say about it.'

'Science?' asked my fellow traveller. 'Of which science do you speak?'

'Well, I meant modern science.'

'Ah, that is what you meant,' he said. 'Yes, that science has nothing to say of such things. Nothing that can be taken seriously at any rate.'

'Is there another science then, in your view?' I asked cautiously, in case my growing hunch might be mistaken.

'But certainly there is,' he said, and gave me a significant look that seemed to say, 'You need not be anxious and ask superfluous questions.'

'The other science,' he went on, 'penetrates the depths of existence that are composed entirely of spirit. This, compared to ordinary science, is reading as opposed to just spelling.'

Now I felt sure ground beneath my feet.

'And so you know of spiritual science and Rudolf Steiner?'

'Spiritual science came to birth for millennia. Steiner was its creator and at the same time its first martyr.'

'Then we can speak openly,' I said, relieved and pleased.

'I would be very glad to do so,' said the sonorous voice.

A stewardess offered us drinks. I chose a coffee and water, while my companion declined. Two rows forward from us, a passenger was watching a football match on a screen.

'The populace-unifying sport of today,' I said, somewhat ironically. 'Millions succumb to it.'

'Yet football is not a chance phenomenon of the times,' said my companion.

'In what way?' I asked curiously.
'Well, we're living in the Piscean age, are we not?'
My interest grew.
'In the last Piscean age, the human being first set *his foot* on earth's solid ground.'
'At the end of the Lemurian period...' I remarked. 'Today people still visit the place on Adam's Peak—Sri Lanka's holy mountain—where Adam left his footprint.'
'Yes, I have been there,' said the other. 'A fine legend, and at the same time more than mere legend. This occurred in the seventh era of Lemurian times.' And after a brief silence he added: 'The foot is the will organ for our work on earth.'
'And what does this have to do with football today?'
'Today, as you know full well, we must place ourselves *spiritually* on our own feet.' He gave me another significant look.
'Most people have an inkling of this,' I said, spinning the thread further, 'yet the materialism of today makes them focus only on their *physical* feet. And so they go busily about the world, and, for entertainment or recreation, they play or watch—football.'
'That's how it is,' he agreed. 'The football craze is not only big business, but a caricature too, and a counter-image of the spiritual feet we need to develop in this modern Piscean age.'
On the screen a little way in front of us, joyful leaps and grimaces revealed that one side had just beaten the other.
'People have scarcely any sense of the spiritual victory granted to someone who seeks true freedom and independence.' There was a touch of sadness now in my companion's voice. 'The phrase "standing on one's own

two feet" is remarkably apt for this condition of self-reliance.'

*

Over the intercom came the captain's voice: 'We are just flying over Rome now, as our passengers on the left side will see.'

'Shame that we're sitting on the wrong side,' I quipped. 'Rome, the eternal city...'

'I would tend to describe it rather as the city of iron resistance to the new spiritual Word,' said my interlocutor calmly. 'Did you know that the works of Steiner are also being examined down there, not only with negative appraisal. The two last Popes have been very assiduous students of anthroposophy, in fact, one giving it very warm attention, the other scrutinizing it with a cold heart...'

'But surely Steiner's teachings are ultimately regarded there as mistaken,' I interjected.

'Indeed, and yet they agree with him in almost every respect,' he opined. 'They think his only mistake was to have given utterance to his teachings *prematurely*, because people were not yet ready for them.'

'Is this just an error? Or an evil stratagem to preserve their own power?' I asked.

'Not easy to answer that. But very few will actually know they are lying when they state this... Most of the clerics down there,'—and here my companion pointed downwards through the cabin floor to the city we had just flown over—'simply do not know that the science of the spirit belongs to *our* Piscean age in the same way that the departure of the moon belonged to the *last* one.'

'And yet,' I objected, 'the history of the spiritual movement after Steiner's death surely testifies to immaturity amongst many of his followers.'

My companion turned his face to me, looked me deep in the eyes, and said very seriously: 'That is how it appears. But Steiner knew that all abuse of his spiritual teachings by immature souls was, ultimately, the lesser evil compared with the concealment of esoteric knowledge by the Church and the whole of derailed Freemasonry. If these things had remained secret, humanity would have been helplessly exposed to evil. Steiner had an unshakeable knowledge that our Piscean age requires humanity to recognize and perceive evil so as to be able to subsequently transform it.'

'And this evil can only be recognized, opposed and transformed by spiritual means,' I said.

'Correct,' said the other, seemingly entirely disregarding this intentional detour I had made to arrive at what was for me a foregone conclusion.

The next moment we were offered a small snack. Since my neighbour declined, I did the same. The conversation was too precious, and our time was limited.

'Do you know the movement started by Joseph Smith?' I asked, seeking to broaden the discussion.

'Oh yes, surely no one can overlook it if they perceive the times aright. Currently it is becoming part of the shield, and its toxic barb, which the Church and decadent Freemasonry forge to fend off the new Word of spirit.'

'We are dealing here with a world-historical rhythm,' I said, 'which proceeds from Gondishapur through the destruction of the Templar Order to the attempt to suppress the new spiritual Word.'

'The third wave of Sorath since the physical appearance,'

and here the voice of my companion grew quieter, 'of Christ upon this planet.'

'The Sorath rhythm, to which the Apocalypse already refers.'

'Yes indeed, this rhythm is working itself out at present, now, in our day. The Sorath rhythm. Sorath is attempting to prepare Ahriman's incarnation — of which you know much — in a way that will go unobserved.'

'"The mystic light on earth is burning me," says Ahriman in Steiner's fourth play — "I must continue working there..."'

'"...without the mystics revealing all my works,"' added my interlocutor, word for word without hesitation. 'But that is the great task for all who seriously seek to nurture and promulgate Steiner's movement in future — to reveal the present ploys of Ahriman.'

At my questioning silence, my companion continued: 'You see, you spoke of Gondishapur — which embodied the battle against the true spirit of Aristotelianism. And you spoke of the destruction of the Templars — the battle against esoteric Christianity. Today we have on our hands the battle against the substance of the new Word of spirit. And this battle too has its earthly anchorage.'

'Gondishapur, Paris, and...?'

'Silicon Valley and Salt Lake City,' he continued. And after a long pause he added: 'The first of these is the dwelling place of intellectual knowledge chained to electrical power; the second is the point of departure for an attempt to eradicate the spiritual substance of the new Word of spirit.'

'I understand,' I said, though struck more than comprehending.

'One night soon after Steiner's death, an advanced pupil of the martyred initiate had a visionary experience. She saw the infertile salt lake region with humanoid beings that appeared to her to be entirely mineral- and plantlike in nature. Then she saw her teacher passing through the land with a group of his pupils, to kindle it to new life. But against him stormed a host of these beings, and their battle cry was, "Mor-mon, Mor-mon." This picture is becoming reality today.'

'As far as I know, Steiner only once suggested an approximate name that Ahriman might bear as an inconspicuous citizen...'

'John William Smith,' said my companion.

'Joseph Smith—John William Smith—a remarkable similarity...'

'Which suggests,' he said, 'that the movement started by Smith—a grotesque caricature of all legitimate religious revelations in humanity's history—is acting to further Ahriman's aims.'

'But how do you interpret the positive and in some places enthusiastic adoption into our movement of the intellectualized picture of the spirit Word and its originator which has come from Salt lake City?'

'How do you interpret this yourself?' he asked me in a friendly tone.

'I interpret it as an effect of the spiritual fog with which Sorath and Ahriman seek to shroud any vestiges of the substance of the new spirit Word.'

'Are you speaking from experience?'

'Yes, I am,' I said. 'While I was never an opponent of this new Word of the spirit, Sorath can also act at other levels in distorting and destructive ways.' I hoped that my questioner would not notice that I was visibly blushing as I recalled experiences that now rose vividly before me.

My companion was silent. Then he asked another question: 'You have visited Caltabelotta have you not?'

At my silent nod, he said: 'Then you have seen the workshop of Klingsor and also know the secret of the dead inclusions or enclaves in the physical and etheric body?'

'Certainly. I am seeking deeper insight into these things at present.'

'You see,' he continued, 'this spiritual fog you spoke of penetrates through these enclaves in the lower bodies into the souls of those who can be befuddled — the great majority of mankind today. But most at risk are those who are meant to create true reception for the message of the spirit. They do not sufficiently feel, think and act out of the I, the source of spiritual independence. One always feels like crying out to them, 'Protect yourselves from what rises from your lower bodies. Warm through and illumine your I,' — and here once more his voice grew quieter — 'through the presence of the Christ I.'

'How do prospects look for the future?' I dared ask after long reflection.

'Well, our friend, the great initiator of the new Word of spirit' — and here it seemed to me he spoke the word 'our' with an almost unnoticeable emphasis — 'once said to one of his closest pupils, 'Never forget that humanity is dancing on a volcano.' Today this phrase needs to be slightly modified.' The stranger turned his face to me, looked me in the eye with a serious and at the same time benevolent glance, and said: 'Today we should say instead that *humanity is walking through burning lava*. This lava consists of materialistic feelings and habits of thought, of unbridled passions and the powers of evil that rise up from the earth's interior.'

Conversation on the Flight Home   43

'How can we survive this?' I asked spontaneously.

'Let me first answer your question with a true anecdote. A great explorer, who was at the same time a great occultist, once descended deep into the mines of Cornwall. He had to abseil down. As it grew ever hotter in the depths, he said to his guide, "It's getting hotter and hotter down here. Tell me: how far before we reach the regions of hell?" At this the man replied: "If you let go of the rope you'll be there in seconds."' We both laughed. Then my companion commented, 'Yes, if you take yourself too seriously you'll soon be lost; if you have no sense of humour, and can't smile at your own weaknesses, you'll get stuck in yourself.' And then, more seriously, in deliberate yet at the same time encouraging tones: 'You see, today everything depends on making your spiritual feet invulnerable by both raising yourself to the heights and plumbing the depths through spirit knowledge, tirelessly strengthening your trust as you do so, in the bright, warm I that remains inviolable.' And after a brief pause he added: 'Like Hieram—or I could also say, like Empedocles—people must hurl themselves into the depths to discover their intact and inviolable core.'

*

A new intercom message interrupted our dialogue. 'Ladies and gentlemen, we will shortly be landing at Basel. Please do not use the toilets now but return to your seats, lock the tray tables in an upright position and fasten your seat belts.'

My companion rose, his gentle eyes smiling warmly at me, and slowly moved forward down the aisle towards the front of the plane. I assumed he would return in a minute or two, and looked forward to continuing the conversation.

I waited and waited. The seat beside me remained empty. I looked around several times—no sign of him. Strange thoughts began to go through my head—didn't the stranger bear a similarity to...? Or to...? But no, it was impossible! Had I been dreaming? Was I dreaming now? I pinched my own hand to make sure I was awake. But then I felt a warm tranquillity flowing through me, and knew I had not been dreaming.

The plane landed. 'Ladies and gentlemen,' crackled the intercom again, 'thank you for flying with Easyjet, and we hope to welcome you aboard again soon. Please leave the aircraft by the front or rear exit. And please make sure you have all your belongings with you.'

I rose from my seat and joined the end of a small queue that was slowly moving towards the rear exit.

'Excuse me, sir, there's an envelope left on your seat—it must be yours,' said an air hostess.

'Oh, thanks very much,' I said distractedly; and there indeed lay a small white envelope. I picked it up. On it, in fine, clear handwriting, stood the words: 'To the friend of the new Word of the spirit.' I opened it, found there a small sheet of paper, and read, in somewhat smaller letters:

Today the phrase that guides our development is this:

Barefoot through burning lava

And below this, in still smaller script, were the words:

Always your unknown friend

I put the sheet carefully back into the envelope with a sense of wonder, then placed the envelope in my jacket pocket and was the last passenger to leave the aeroplane.

II

The unforeseen circumstances of my return journey, especially my encounter with the stranger, went on reverberating in me for a long time. Slowly but surely they were asking for continuation, or some kind of conclusion to the whole undertaking. Or at least some of the planted seeds needed to ripen further.

On 23 April I once again flew past Etna, which greeted me like an old friend, though not as conspicuously as on the first occasion. Its upper part was white this time, snow-covered. From its head hung only a flat pigtail of cloud that faded into the distance.

On the day of Shakespeare's birth and death, and the birthday of Ludwig Polzer-Hoditz, I arrived on Sicilian soil again, in Catania. In England this day is celebrated as St George's Day; and in Sicily the whole island celebrates San Giorgio with colourful processions. I took this fact as the motif for my journey.

Milazzo

The minibus hurtled along towards Milazzo, thankfully without incident. From here I was to visit the volcanic island of Stromboli. Since there was no time left that day to make the crossing by ship, I toured the harbour town. High above Milazzo, as on a throne, sits the fortress established by the Arabs, developed by the Staufer dynasty under

Frederick II, and then expanded further by the Bourbons and the Spaniards. It is said to be Frederick II's mightiest fortress in all Sicily, though not the most beautiful. *Might* is perhaps the most accurate word to sum up the history of this city.

*

The path up to the fortress started at the harbour avenue Lungomare Garibaldi, and led past stone tablets in memory of the decisive victory which Giuseppe Garibaldi won here on 20 July 1860 with his 'army of a thousand' against the Bourbons. This victory was the real starting point for Italy's unification, which began here in Sicily. I couldn't help thinking of the harbourside house in Nizza that I had visited a few days previously, where, as a memorial plaque announced, Garibaldi's birth house had once stood. The son of an ordinary sailor, he was born in Nizza and won the great victory of his life here in Milazzo. These two places are therefore the most important emblems of his earthly destiny.

Almost exactly a whole cultural epoch (2160) years earlier, another battle had been waged just outside Milazzo: the Roman fleet under Consul Caius Julius Duilius vanquished the Carthaginians, thus ending the first Punic war in 260 BC. In those days Milazzo was called Mylae. The victory of Mylae led to the eventual destruction of Carthage in 146 BC, and thus to the rise of Rome as a seafaring and world empire. Duilius had developed a technique whereby the Romans, hitherto the underdogs at sea, could board enemy vessels with a boarding bridge, conquering the Carthaginians on, as it were, their own 'territory'. In connection with the decisive surprise attack

Milazzo   47

on Luettich at the beginning of the First World War, Rudolf Steiner speaks of the battle of Mylae and this Roman stratagem. He hints at a karmic relationship between Duilius and Ludendorff, in whose soul there still remained a non-Christian quality.

Both battles at Milazzo smoothed the way for new impulses of world-historical importance. Mylae prepared Rome's mission in the world, and Milazzo that of Italy's unification. These battles both took place in the shadow of the Liparian Islands, which—especially Stromboli—are still volcanically active.

The path to the fortress also led past a memorial bearing the image of a goddess of conquest and holding the torch of freedom aloft, reminiscent of the Statue of Liberty in New York harbour. We can see good reason for the fact that a 'goddess' rather than Garibaldi himself stands here in celebration of his achievements. From his former life as a Hibernian initiate, Giuseppe Garibaldi brought far more than merely personal aims with him when he descended to his life on earth. Alongside him, as is well known, worked other individuals who, according to Steiner's esoteric research, were *all* pupils of Garibaldi in the Hibernian Mysteries: Camillo Benso di Cavour, Giuseppe Mazzini and Victor Emanuel.[8] On 22 March 1924, Steiner explained that Garibaldi, a teacher in the Hibernian Mysteries in an earlier incarnation, was obliged in a later incarnation to serve and follow his former pupils.[9] It is therefore understandable why the very Republican-minded Garibaldi nevertheless allowed Victor Emanuel to found a monarchy. That this karmic *group* was needed to unite Italy also shows us that the unification was not only very important but also had to be pushed through against great resistance. What, one wonders, would have become of the influence of Klingsor in Sicily if this island had gone its own way?

I passed through the fortress gate thinking about these two great battles of world history. As I bought my entrance ticket, I asked about a guided tour, and also about Garibaldi, expecting to get a positive response.

'Garibaldi! Don't speak to us about Garibaldi! Nor that Eugene of Savoy, who put on grand airs and drove the Bourbons from the land.'

'You mean that Sicily would have been better off if the Bourbons had gone on ruling?'

The dialogue ended abruptly with a very definite 'yes' to this question. Seldom had I witnessed such a collision between deeds of historical necessity and the prevalent human desire to keep everything as it was. If the Garibaldi memorial at Lungomare Garibaldi is ever defaced, I imagine that certain draconian forces in the neighbourhood will be behind it. Alerted by this disparagement of historical realities, before I continued my travels I couldn't help touching on the theme again at the hotel reception desk. 'Garibaldi—what's so special about *him*?' said the young man writing out my bill. 'Just a man like anyone else,' he added. Garibaldi destroyed the dream here of a Sicily independent of Italy. The island seems to have no separatist hero for people to rally around, like, say, Robert the Bruce, who is so dear a figure to Scotland's independence movement.

Reflecting on the perpetual conflict between retrograde and progressive impulses in human history, the next morning I boarded the ferry for Stromboli.

Stromboli

On our arrival the rain was bucketing down, followed by lightning and thunder. After a short halt I set out for Osservatorio, which also houses a pizzeria. Then the sun came out again, and the clouds drifted away. The path first led along the seashore, then along a narrow alley between mostly one-storey white houses in which no one seemed to be living. I had an occasional view of the shimmering ocean. A handful of guests sat in the terrace restaurant, each looking expectantly up towards the summit of the volcano from which rose, at short intervals, grey, brown or black plumes of smoke. Tripods were fetched and placed in position. But only now and then did the volcano emit a dark tower of smoke. After sunset it got noticeably cooler. I had sat down at table number 23, as I learned when the waiters called my order into the kitchen (23, the date of my arrival, is also that of some very important anniversaries).

The stars came out. There was Mercury too (often mistaken for Venus), Jupiter, and between these the waxing moon. Then later Sirius, Betelgeuse and Regulus in Leo. The volcano quietly emitted its streamers of smoke into the growing darkness, and these gradually formed something like a milky way between the ever more numerous stars. Then suddenly a red fountain of sparks. Happy relief spread over the terrace. Altogether one could sense a kind of reverent awe amongst the people waiting there, and gratitude for the least sign of smoke or fire from the mountain. Then everything fell very silent again—so silent that one could almost hear the stars. The beginning of a mantram from *Der Meditationweg der Michaelschule* ('Meditative Path of the Michael School') passed through my mind: 'Cosmic sanctuaries of the stars / the dwellings of the gods...' Palaces of the gods! How often we gaze up to them — but rarely with the right sense of wonder. Is there anything else so lofty and sublime to which we can lift our eyes from so many places in the world? Did we not gaze up to Sirius in Egyptian, Greek and medieval times? And now we do so again! From different bodily eyes our soul has repeatedly looked upon one and the same star, and in doing so was visited by one or another of the communities of the gods. This we have forgotten.

And now, again, a red fire flames from the volcano, like a flash of memory of something long forgotten that we once experienced. Can we stay sitting when the stars begin to speak?

*

A trip around the island? Why not? I had half a day to spare before my excursion to the crater region. I went out into the freshening wind and moderate waves in a comfortable rubber dinghy. The only others with me were a couple from Vienna visiting Stromboli for the third time. Our guide, a native Strombolian, also married to a Viennese woman, showed and explained to us everything he thought important — such as the 'Scari', the mountain's eastern flank where much lava has descended, as was apparent from the now crumbling brown-black rockface that falls around 700 metres into the ocean. At that moment, as if in confirmation, the volcano stack suddenly spewed a black-grey cloud into the sky. We were told about the olive and caper cultivation that was finished off by a big eruption in the 1930s; and there used to be wine-growing too. Many of the inhabitants emigrated. The island had never been populous anyway. And now it fell into a kind of Sleeping Beauty dormancy, from which it was woken by the Italian film director Rosselini who in 1949 made the film *Stromboli* with Ingrid Bergmann. Tourism began, and today is the chief income for the islanders.

We briefly visited the little village of Ginostra on the western flank, where Indians and Pakistanis had once settled. We walked through the narrow twisting, climbing and plunging lanes, breathing the wonderful stillness and looking far off to a view of the other islands. Then we travelled onwards. The 'Sciara dei Fuoco' on the west flank is even bigger and more imposing than the 'Sciara' on the east side, and also descends right down to the sea. On the solitary rockstack of Strombolicchio, on which stands a lighthouse, our guide showed us natural formations and rock profiles in which people's imagination has discerned all kinds of other things: a heart, the head of a horse, and a Picasso portrait! We were shown a cemetery placed well away from the biggest village: mostly child victims of the cholera which raged here after the Second World War. Then we passed whitewashed cubes of houses, which would not have been out of place in Tunisia, and reached our starting point again. Before we arrived at our destination, I asked why, yesterday, there had been a great tanker anchored close to the edge of the village, connected by a tube to the land. 'It's the water supply for the island,' replied our guide. 'It comes from Reggio di Calabria, once or twice a week.' He said it was the same for all the Liparian islands. 'Water, water, everywhere, and not a drop to drink...' Obvious now you think about it, but paradoxical somehow.

The Workshop of Hephaestus

A touring Dutchman told me the evening before that the ascent was 'tough', but I didn't let this scare me off. The next day my guide cast a knowledgeable eye over my equipment and found everything wanting except my boots. I was lent a good rucksack, a helmet and a lamp attached to the latter. The tour started at 4 p.m. and was to last until 10 p.m. The group of around 20 people from many different countries set off punctually, ascending in a long, orderly queue. We had 900 metres to climb to the summit. My lungs were having to work harder than usual while most of the others in the party looked like they were taking a leisurely Sunday stroll. The guide seemed concerned about me, giving me an encouraging thumbs-up every now and then. After a while he ordered me to the head of the group, since a team, he said, can't go faster than its slowest member. As we ascended he broke off a tree branch with practised skill, broke this into two and gave me one of them as a walking stick. I was reminded again of my ascent of Adam's Peak in Sri Lanka, which had been similarly exhausting for someone as unfit as I am.

After around three hours, the group arrived at the summit shortly before sunset, as planned: the view was exhilarating. Then we heard a rumble, familiar to me from Etna. 'The mountain is greeting us,' I said to the guide, who nodded in cheerful confirmation. A smell of phosphorus became apparent. A few more steps and we found ourselves about 100 metres above the crater, from which plumes of smoke were rising. As the sun set in the distance, our view below came into sharper focus: the red magma began to shine in the main crater from which the smoke was seething. It felt as if we were gazing down into the workshop of Hephaestus, the world still emerging and developing from fire. Uniquely on earth, I reflected, something of the earth's primordial development is here preserved and perpetuated in *continuous* Strombolian activity, sometimes more, sometimes less intense — something of ancient evolution continuing throughout all earth's stages from Saturn to Vulcan. Suddenly, to the delight of the expectant watchers, a small fountain of red sparks, a ribbon of magma, rose up and then fell back into the magma womb below.

Like a sudden awakening, the guide's shout of 'andiamo!' brought us back from far, far away — from depths of earth and long spans of time.

We descended in darkness, first crossing one of the large, ash-covered lava fields. It felt like wading through snow, half walking, half sinking. We made quicker progress now than on the ascent, and soon found solid ground under our feet again. Even though these feet of mine were aching more and more, if anyone had asked them they would have said 'wonderful'. But once is enough. A Frenchman, who seemed to feel the same, quipped, 'Ça valait la peine — littéralement!'[*]

But all the small discomforts will fade from memory, leaving that gift of the sight of the ever-active forge where earth and man emerge from fire.

The subtitle of Rossellini's film was *Terra di Dio*. He was right. Who could deny God, having gazed into such primordial depths of the world?

*

---

[*] 'That was worth the trouble/pain — literally!'

Before I fell asleep I heard the news that Nepal had been hit by a devastating earthquake, with thousands of victims, many injured, countless homes destroyed. Yes, the earth quakes: it lives and feels, and in sublime and ghastly form it reflects what lives in the human soul—though of course not always at the precise location where the human soul most forcefully erupts. There are surrogate wars, and perhaps also surrogate victims of natural disaster. But in global terms, the earth's interior holds up to our inner soul a grandiose or also terrible mirror of self-knowledge. Who looks into it? Who even begins to think of natural spectacles such as those of Stromboli, or disasters such as the one in Nepal, as true mirrors of our inner condition?

Palermo

The railway line from Milazzo to Palermo mostly follows the coast and offers fine views of little towns, pebbly strands and the great ocean. The train halted at every station, collecting more and more people. By the time we got to Cefalú, the train was full to bursting, and passengers had to stand in a dense crush. But everything was curiously quiet. Until Palermo you could almost have heard a pin drop, as if the whole train was holding its breath. Who would have thought that so many people in such a small space would have been so quiet in Italy?

I was reading Martin-Ingbert Heigl's remarkable book 'Persephone—Goethe's Italian Trip to the Archetypes, and the Essence of Anthroposophy'.[*] I discovered here that a

---

[*] *Persephone—Goethes Reise zu den Urbildern und das Wesen der Anthroposophie.*

significant stage in finding the archetypal plant had not taken place in the Botanical garden in Palermo — which did not yet exist — but in the fine gardens of the Villa Giuglia close by. I sought out this park on my arrival, and found it almost empty of people. At its centre stood a sundial in the form of a pentagonal dodecahedron, and around it a circle inside a square, in turn within a larger square turned 45 degrees, all bisected by two diagonals and surrounded by cross-shaped paths. Not far away from this stood an allegorical sculpture of the spirit of the city of Palermo. Here again there was unwonted quiet. And the loveliest scents and fragrances, including orange blossom.

Statues were everywhere, decaying and yet charming. I lay down on a stone bench and fell into a doze, from which I was woken by a few drops of rain.

When Goethe visited here in April 1787, the 'old whim', as he called it, surfaced in him again: the great idea of the archetypal plant. But this 'idea he saw with his eyes' only came to full spiritual birth in Naples. In the gardens in Palermo he was still hoping to find it as one of the actual physical plants surrounding him here.

The midwife of the true form of the archetypal plant was an experience that shook Goethe awake to the reality of the elemental world. This was his sea crossing to Naples, on his return from Sicily, in May of that year. The ship was at risk from a strong current that could have smashed it against the cliffs of Capri. Panic broke out amongst the passengers. Goethe walked among them and soothed the 'soul storm', having in mind the action of Christ on Lake Tiber, which he sought to conjure in his words. The situation calmed and changed. All was redeemed. It is worth reading about this experience in Goethe's *Italian*

Journey. It led him to the *living* quality of the archetypal plant, which until then had remained a more abstract concept. Here in the gardens of Villa Giuglia — perhaps in tranquillity as deep as I enjoyed today — Goethe may have begun to expand the scope of his reflections as a prelude to this, his greatest scientific discovery. Of these public gardens he himself said: 'It is the most wonderful place in the world. While formally planted, it nevertheless seems fairylike in character' (7 April 1787).

Cagliostro, Goethe and Steiner

Looking through a list of restaurants for somewhere to eat, my eye fell on one called 'Le Delizie di Cagliostro' in Via Vittorio Emanuele.

The name of this much maligned 'magician', whom I had studied extensively after the first stage of this trip, had an immediate effect on me. I was the first customer to enter the restaurant that evening. On the wall hung a colour portrait of Cagliostro, and above the counter were two Italian books about him. It was irresistable. Quickly I chose from the menu, then asked if I might take a look at the books. The hors d'oeuvre came. I ate — and read — and must have been a strange sight. The glances of the waiters seemed to convey a mixture of amusement and surprise. They must have thought I was more interested in their Cagliostro books than in the food they brought me. I had immersed myself in the thin volume by Giuseppe Quatriglio, *Il Romanzo di Cagliostro*. The book bore a handwritten dedication from the author to the restaurant's owners. Before I had finished the main course, I had read the brief chapter on Goethe. We know of Goethe's visit to the family of Joseph Balsamo, originally from Palermo, whom he, like many others, believed to be the real figure behind 'Cagliostro'. Goethe regarded this occultist, who got mixed up in the scurrilous 'necklace affair', as a charlatan and a swindler. With the help of a legal expert who was also investigating the business, Goethe approached Balsamo's family, introduced himself under a false name, and brought them invented news from Balsamo solely in order to find out information. From Weimar Goethe even sent the poor family the 14 gold pieces which they said were owed them by 'Cagliostro'—whom Goethe had seemingly traced. In his play *The Grand Kofta*, he also left him a notable memorial.

It is brilliantly written and apt for all false gurus, of those times or today—but not true of the real Cagliostro. To acknowledge the real nature of this figure, says Steiner in his only reference to the 'much maligned' Cagliostro, 'whom few recognized', is possible only for highly initiated occultists. In the same lecture he also says important things about the Count of St Germain.[10] According to Steiner, Cagliostro led his pupils to an understanding of the human being's invisible bodies through inner work on the pentagram. He was highly benevolent, healed people without payment, worked for a long time in Strasbourg and Basel, and appeared to enjoy great good fortune. In Basel, he was a frequent visitor to the Sarasins and here, as elsewhere, he undertook high-level Freemasonry work. The pavilion given to him near the Beyeler Museum in Riehen is still there today. But envy also followed at his heels. When a doctor challenged him to a duel, Cagliostro proposed that instead of crudely trying to shoot each other the duellers should give each other poison. The victor would be the one who possessed the better antidote. His opponent declined and was declared the loser. Cagliostro's end in the dungeons of the Vatican is shrouded in mystery. It can scarcely be seen as a karmic recompense for former deeds, but rather as a germ of later developments that arise through suffering *undeserved* injustice.

*

One hundred years later, Helena Petrovna Blavatsky was similarly villainized. She was the great innovator of a new spiritual world-view which the times required, and, very importantly, smoothed the way for the work of Rudolf Steiner. The latter knew her imperfections, but he valued her never-wavering trust in the great 'Masters of Wisdom and of the Harmony of Feelings'. He respected her thorough truthfulness, above all towards herself and her own weaknesses. It is said that Blavatsky wore Cagliostro's ring. Certainly she possessed his sense of truth. Franz Hartmann, for a period a close colleague of Blavatsky, once asked her for a portrait of herself. Without a word she produced, in answer, a portrait of Cagliostro. Emil Bock once remarked to a fellow priest that he was convinced that the two were connected through reincarnation. In this light, Cagliostro's martyrdom at the end of his life appears as *preparation* for the still greater martyrdom that Blavatsky had to endure when she was denigrated for years for her spiritual world mission.

*

Goethe brought back with him from Sicily two important fruits: his deeper insight into the archetypal plant, and, as mentioned earlier in relation to the figure of Empedocles, important seeds for the second part of *Faust*. The third went awry. His search for 'Cagliostro' led nowhere. He himself misled it when, as he recounts, he introduced himself to the Balsamo family as an Englishman, though he does not divulge the pseudonym he used.

In strange contrast to this manhunt fiasco, a few days before his first visit to the Balsamo family, and likewise in Palermo, someone spoke to him about the author of *Werther*, at which he revealed himself to be its writer! Goethe feigned acquaintance with the person he was seeking, but this was insufficient to identify who the latter actually was. According to Quatriglio, the real Cagliostro is said to have responded to all suspicions about his identity by stating: 'Pour savoir çe qu'il est, il faudrait être lui-même.'* This was too difficult for Goethe, despite his almost unbounded capacity for sympathy. Only Steiner was able to accomplish it, through the *true insight of Intuition*, which, without losing one's own I, is capable of merging with the spiritual core of another human being.

Without Steiner's karmic research into Cagliostro, we might regard Goethe's Balsamo enquiries as the third fruit of his trip to Sicily. A great genius may also commit grave errors. The Spirit of Palermo, whose statue still greets the visitor to the gardens of Villa Giuglia, will have observed this very noteworthy and instructive mistake by Goethe— until Rudolf Steiner was able to transform it into a profound and enigmatic truth.

---

*'To know what he is, it would be necessary to be him.'

Parsifal in Palermo

In the Grand Hotel et Des Palmes where I spent my last two nights, Richard Wagner once stopped — a fact widely advertised here. He was staying in Palermo between November 1881 and January 1882 to finish the score of *Parsifal*, which cost him a great deal of laborious work. Plagued by health problems, he sought to recuperate by reading Shakespeare or going on outings with his family — to the gardens of Villa Giuglia, or to Monreale, which he repeatedly visited. But his real recuperation came from every completed page of the score. Thus the destiny of this work, infused with the essence of his artistic and spiritual credo, is also strongly connected with Palermo. In the second of the three acts of this grand and moving work, Klingsor's power reaches its culmination when he compels Kundry to tempt and thus destroy the strongest of the Grail knights. In the same act Parsifal wrests the stolen spear from him and so breaks the whole spell Klingsor has woven.

In the middle of this dramatic second act is the terrifying and sublime moment when Parsifal, almost succumbing to Kundry's temptation, suddenly perceives in true Intuition the nature of Amfortas's suffering. 'The wound!' he calls out when this vision dawns in him at last — as, after all his errors, he gains 'knowledge through sympathy'. The score that sought to put this spiritual victory into music had to be completed in Sicily.

Phanuel and Enoch

The Palatine Chapel is concealed behind the blunt and unlovely exterior of the Norman palace. The chapel was incorporated into the large palace in a brief period between 1132 and 1140 by the brilliant Roger II of Sicily. It is the 'Sainte-Chapelle' of Palermo. As modest as this is in its proportions and dimensions, it leads the visitor not into a stained glass feast of colour but into a sea of mosaic images: it spans the biblical narrative from the Creation of the world to the mission of Israel entrusted to Jacob. We are all familiar with the story of Jacob wrestling with the angel – 'I will not let thee go, except thou bless me,' says Jacob, the spiritual combatant, to the angel. The angel blesses him and gives him the new name, 'Israel'. But here, in the Palatine Chapel, the angel also bears a name – Phanuel. It is only here that he is so named. In the almost identical depiction at Monreale he remains unnamed – unnamed and usually also entirely unrecognized.

I was gripped by the sight of this image of the angel wrestling with Jacob, and the birth of the mission of Israel to which Phanuel gave spiritual blessing. I sat down on the pew closest to the sanctuary so as to give myself up to it without interruption from the stream of tourists that moved slowly through the chapel like a single flow of lava, engulfing everything in its way. The apocryphal Book of Enoch refers to Phanuel and describes him. And in a lecture on 20 April 1908 (GA 102), Rudolf Steiner said that 'he was the guardian called upon by those who sought initiation'. Jacob is therefore here presented as an *initiate*. But who, I pondered, was Enoch, a figure knowledgeable enough to speak of the 'angel of initiation'?

'Enoch was none other than the spiritual teacher whom you follow,' said a voice behind me. I knew at once to whom it belonged. Turning round, I looked into the friendly, smiling eyes of my stranger.

'A son of Cain,' he added quietly.

'Rudolf Steiner incarnated as Enoch?' I asked him as quietly.

'To one of his pupils Steiner once said, in passing: "...when I was Enoch..."'

This revelation was so unexpected and far-reaching that at first I forgot the strange fact of meeting the stranger here again. I rose to my feet slowly, went to the row behind and sat down in the empty seat next to him.

'And you,' I said quietly, almost in a whisper, 'who are *you*?'

'The composer you so revere, who also wrote and composed *Lohengrin*.' And after a brief pause he added: 'Do *you* understand?'

'I understand,' I said spontaneously, although only the faintest understanding was dawning on me.

'I can only continue accompanying those who do not ask too quickly about my nature and origins. Later they will learn of them.'

An inexpressible silence followed, in which worlds seemed to revolve.

'In the meantime you visited the ever-active Stromboli and gazed into the forge of the volcano,' the stranger continued. 'From its fire all true sons of Cain must strike the sparks from which new spiritual fire can be kindled.' His countenance became grave and thoughtful, and he said: 'Today it is usually only *soul* fires that flare.'

'And spiritual interest usually flashes out only once, at most, like the cameras here,' I added.

'That is so. But only those whose feet become invulnerable can find their way to the spirit fire.' I had to think of my own sore, aching feet as I was coming down from Stromboli.

'I am speaking only of the *spiritual* feet that can wade through soul lava,' added the stranger.

I patted my breast pocket to show by mime that I had well understood the message that my unknown friend had left me on my flight back, and that since then it was always close to my heart. He understood, and smiled.

'And Phanuel?' I asked, after this silent exchange.

'He is a brother of Michael. He works with spirit gold but also with the star iron of his brother spirit. He lends invulnerability to spiritual feet as they make the transition into the realm of spiritual reality.' And then, after a pause, he added: 'Phanuel remains the angel of initiation to this day. He guards what is unspoiled and indestructible within us. Or rather, he helps draw up to the surface of the soul what has remained pure in us, for it is only this that can cross the threshold to the world of spirit. Spiritual science also calls him the "Guardian of the Threshold".'

I looked up involuntarily to the wrestling Jacob.

After a long silence, my unknown friend said: 'Never forget that now individuals, and later the whole of humanity, must pass before Phanuel—just as they once passed him in Lemurian times as they were released into the world of the senses. Back then, the sleeping human being was discharged downwards; today he must battle his way back upwards consciously. But Phanuel only now blesses those who are first prepared to wade barefoot through burning soul lava.'

'But how can people actually learn to do this?' I asked, thinking of the soul lava with which I was all too familiar. 'They have far more of the flaws of Amfortas in them than the insights of Parsifal.'

'There are many things that can help,' said the stranger

with a warmth in his voice that encouraged me. 'But three things above all: *reflecting on earthly afflictions, love for earthly values and spirit-devoted earthly will.* Those who develop these virtues do not need to worry about their spiritual feet.'

Then came words from a loudspeaker: 'Visitors are requested to make their way towards the exit. The chapel will close in a few minutes.' The small lava stream of tourists ponderously but inexorably flowed past us. I had been attending to them as little as to the previous announcements that must have come through the loud-speaker.

'And Enoch-Steiner?' I asked cautiously, turning my face towards the stranger.

In our Piscean age he is the greatest helper of Phanuel, the Guardian of the Threshold to the world of spirit. Many of his pupils are pleased to speak of Michael. But few — and now the stranger emphasized every single word — earnestly seek to pass the gateway of Phanuel, *the only portal to true knowledge.*' I silently gave him my assent.

'But there is still something you wish to ask,' said my spiritual friend encouragingly.

'I was wondering why people place so little trust in spiritual guidance in their life.'

'Well, usually they believe that such guidance must manifest in great events and tangible things. We are all led and guided; and we can all discern this in apparently chance events and small coincidences or strokes of fortune. But few pay any attention to such small matters. You see, such guidance is also present in the fact that we have met again here, on this of all days. Do you know today's date?'

I had to think. 'It's 28 April,' I said.

'The day on which, in the year 1140, this precious building was inaugurated. Look, over there is an information sheet about it.' I looked up to a wooden panel on one of the walls, to which indeed a printed sheet appeared to be affixed.

'These are the small, magical occurrences that so enrich our daily life.'

Moved, I asked him, 'Will we see one another again?'

'We will. But when and where must be left to higher guidance. Farewell!'

With these words, the stranger gave me a look full of warmth and benevolence, as he placed his index finger on his lips. I understood, and looked up once again to Phanuel. Turning back to my friend again, I found he had gone. Inwardly, it seemed to me I heard the words, 'I can only return again to those who let me depart unquestioningly.'

Recent Earthquakes

On my last evening walk I passed beggars as in the morning, mostly outside churches. A woman was carrying a board on which the words were written: 'No one is helping me.'

Throughout the world earthquakes—greater or smaller in scale—are happening almost every day. Since February 2015 there have been repeated quakes in Chile. In the last week of April there were very severe quakes in Nepal.

In a café I read the latest reports of the extent of the earthquake catastrophe in Nepal—approaching 10,000 victims. My thoughts turned to their sufferings, and to my friends there who are already giving emergency aid and have set up a donation account. The victims of these quakes—and here spiritual science offers true comfort—often receive a kind of impetus for spiritualization of their awareness after death. They have, after all, had a drastic experience of the transience of all physical, earthly existence. The greatest suffering is that of the survivors who, whether injured or not, lose their relatives, friends, homes and belongings.

Next morning, 29 April, I read an article in the *Repubblica* which said something unusual about the catastrophe in Nepal, which had even affected parts of the Himalayas. The Indian writer Anita Nair writes:

> We are egotistically laying waste to the planet; and in our attitude of complete indifference to the rest of humanity, we have contributed to all these catastrophes.

Nair also refers to the fact we mentioned earlier—that many victims of such catastrophes are 'surrogates' for others:

> It strikes me that the people of Nepal have here paid the price for human greed.

These are grandiose thoughts about the shared responsibility of all for the way the planet behaves. Complemented by spiritual-scientific insights into the interior of the earth and its connection with processes at work in the human soul, they can acquire a potency that will not only motivate us to heal material harm, as far as this is possible, but also teach us, finally, to attend to the soul causes of such catastrophes. Nair continues and concludes her article with these words:

The earth does not belong to us, and we cannot do whatever we please. [...] A collective guilt is at work here [...] We must seek a remedy for this guilt.

The remedy has been available for over a hundred years, but very little use is made of it. It is called 'inner development' and spiritual insight into the connection between the human being and the earth'.

Words Heard Within

That afternoon I took a taxi up Mount Pellegrino where there is a shrine to St Rosalia, the patron saint of Palermo. Rosalia died in 1170, the same year Thomas à Becket was murdered in England. So many well-known people had been up here! Goethe, who so much liked the simplicity of the statue of Rosalia, and whose words about it have been carved into stone here; and then also Byron and Cardinal Newman.

Up here a glorious expanse spread out. Below was the Bay of Palermo and the whole city. Good eyes could discern far-off Etna — the mountain that had summoned me. I earnestly asked myself how many future volcanic eruptions there must be, how many earthquakes and similar catastrophes, how many senseless wars testifying only to the denial of the spirit that possesses so many human beings? For how long will humanity have to bring such catastrophes upon itself, or even throw itself thoughtlessly and heartlessly headlong into them?

'For as often and as long,' I heard the now familiar voice saying to me, 'as enough people do not yet seek a spirit-devoted will that wrestles courageously with the catastrophes of life — as Jacob wrestled.'

'How many is "enough"?' I asked inwardly.

From deep stillness within the answer came: 'The number itself does not matter. What matters are the *few* who can help the *many* to kindle within them the eternal spark of the spirit.'

My soul flew back to the Palatine Chapel: to the earthly values preserved within it in such perfect form; to the whole spiritual fabric it enables us to experience; and to everything I had freshly received from the stranger. I was filled with a sense of great gratitude. I felt myself alone, in spiritual community.

Notes

1. Otto Weininger, *Taschenbuch und Briefe an einen Freund*, edited by Artur Geber, Vienna 1922.
2. See Rudolf Steiner's comments in the karma lecture of 23 September 1924 (GA 238). (*Karmic Relationships*, Vol. IV, Rudolf Steiner Press 1983.)
3. See the lecture of 21 September 1924 in GA 238. (Ibid.)
4. See the lecture by Steiner on 7 September 1924, GA 238. (Ibid.)
5. See the lecture of 19 August 1911 in *Weltenwunder, Seelenprüfungen, Geistesoffenbarungen*, GA 129. (*Wonders of the World*, Rudolf Steiner Press 1983.)
6. Hans Gsänger, *Sizilien, Insel des Kains*, Berlin 1956, p. 146.
7. See the lecture by Steiner on 7 February 1913 in *Die Mysterien des Morgenlandes und des Christentums*, GA 144. (*Mysteries of the East and of Christianity*, Rudolf Steiner Press 1972.)
8. Another memorial in Milazzo remembers Mazzini.
9. *Karmic Relationships*, Vol. 1 (Rudolf Steiner Press 1972).
10. Lecture on 16 December 1904, GA 93. (*The Temple Legend*, Rudolf Steiner Press 1985.)